About the Book

Ru Chih Cheo was born in China. Through the difficulties of wartime and in the face of little encouragement from adults, she kept in view the high aspirations she had for herself. Barely out of her teens, she came to America to study science. She went on to become the first woman appointed a full professor in the Science Division of The Johns Hopkins University. Her research on the origin of cancer is respected worldwide.

The story of Ru Chih Cheo Huang tells of a self-reliant girl who planned what she would do to achieve her goal of a happy and fulfilling life.

an American Women in Science biography

Scientist and Planner,
Ru Chih
Cheo Huang

by Mary Ellen Verheyden-Hilliard

drawings by Scarlet Biro

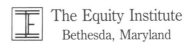

The Equity Institute
Bethesda, Maryland

This work was developed under a grant from the Women's Educational Equity Act Program, U.S. Department of Education. However, the content does not necessarily reflect the position of that Agency and no official endorsement of these materials should be inferred.

Library of Congress Cataloging in Publication Data

Verheyden-Hilliard, Mary Ellen.
    Scientist and planner, Ru Chih Cheo Huang.

    (An American women in science biography)
    Summary: Follows a dedicated woman from her birth in China to her appointment as a full professor in the Science Division of The Johns Hopkins University and discusses her research on the origin of cancer.
    1. Huang, Ru Chih Cheo—Juvenile literature. 2. Women molecular biologists—China—Biography—Juvenile literature. 3. Women molecular biologists—United States—Biography—Juvenile literature. 4. Molecular biologists—China—Biography—Juvenile literature. 5. Molecular biologists—United States—Biography—Juvenile literature. [1. Huang, Ru Chih Cheo. 2. Women molecular biologists. 3. Chinese Americans—Biography] I. Biro, Scarlet, ill. II. Title. III. Series: Verheyden-Hilliard, Mary Ellen. American women in science biography.
QH31.H8V47 1985   574.8'8'0924 [B] [92]   84-25982
ISBN 0-932469-03-5

Scientist and Planner,
Ru Chih
Cheo Huang

Ru Chih carefully dusted the dining room table. It was her duty to keep the house clean. Daughters did housework. Sons did not.

Ru Chih sometimes wished her brothers shared her work, but she did not complain. She just worked faster so she would have enough time to study and play. That's the way things were in China, where Ru Chih and her family lived.

Ru Chih Cheo began her life in China on April 2, 1932. Her father was a college professor. Her mother was a statistician. She used math to collect and understand information. Life for the Cheos was full and rich. Then the war came.

Day after day, the city was bombed. The Cheo family took candles and went to the caves outside the city. There they were safe from bombs. Sometimes they had to stay in the caves for many days and nights.

Ru Chih always felt better once the candles were lit. If I try, I can make the best of anything, Ru Chih said to herself. Someday

the war will be over, and life will
be joyful again.

When the bombing stopped, Ru Chih and her mother would go to get food. Farmers brought food to sell at an outdoor market at the edge of the city.

Sometimes Mrs. Cheo traded one food for another because she did not have any money. She might trade a cup of rice grains for a few fresh vegetables. Sometimes if there was the least little bit left over, Mrs. Cheo would buy a book.

A book was more precious than anything else. Books were filled with stories and pictures and ideas. Ru Chih thought books were the best treat in the market.

Finally, the war was over. Ru Chih could go to school every day instead of sitting in the cave. Ru Chih loved school. There were so many things to do.

Ru Chih liked planning things for everyone to do. Her friends thought she was very good at making plans. They elected her to the student council to help plan things for the whole school.

But what Ru Chih liked best in school was learning math. Solving math problems was like playing a favorite game.

One day in the library, Ru Chih found a book about Dr. Marie Sklodowska Curie, the scientist who discovered X-rays. Ru Chih thought the story of Marie Curie was wonderful. Ru Chih decided she would be a scientist too.

Ru Chih took many science and math classes. She got very good grades. But her teachers did not tell her she was very smart or really encourage her. Ru Chih sometimes wished that they would pay more attention to her, but she was not one to sulk.

"I'll just keep working hard," Ru Chih whispered to herself. "I'll show everyone that I can succeed."

Ru Chih decided she wanted to study science in America. She began to plan how she could achieve her dream. One of her high school teachers had already gone to America. Ru Chih wrote to her teacher and told her of her hopes. Her teacher wrote back that she would help Ru Chih choose a school in America where she could study.

After much planning, Ru Chih was ready for the trip. Her family helped her pack. Finally the day came to leave. Ru Chih said goodbye to her family. Then she got on a ship for the long trip from China to America.

The ocean voyage took many days. As Ru Chih sailed farther and farther from her family, she wondered more and more about America. Would America be like the books she had read about it? Would the people be friendly? Would she be happy in America? It was a little scary to come to a strange land all alone.

Ru Chih's ship landed in California on the west coast of America. Her journey was only half over.

From the ship, Ru Chih went to a bus station and got on a bus. She traveled for six days across the United States. Her college was in Virginia on the east coast of America. She rode through big cities, little towns, and farmland. She saw rivers and mountains and many different kinds of people. She saw more of America in six days than many people see who live in America all their lives. Ru Chih liked what she saw.

When Ru Chih came to America she was just 21 years old. She spoke only a little English. When she started to study science in college she got an "F" on her first science test. But six months later, she got an "A."

In one of her classes, Ru Chih met a young man named Pien Chien Huang. He and Ru Chih fell in love. They went to class together, and they studied together. They both wanted to be scientists.

Ru Chih and Pien Chien graduated from college on the same day. Two hours later they got married!

Being married did not stop Ru Chih from studying. She wanted to earn a doctorate in science. A doctorate is the highest degree a scientist can earn.

In the next four years, Ru Chih earned her doctorate, learned to speak French and German, and had a baby boy! She and her husband named the baby Suber.

Ru Chih and her husband were awarded their doctoral degrees on the same day. Little Suber enjoyed the celebration! In a few years Suber had a sister. Her name is Suzanne.

Now Ru Chih and her husband
are both professors at The Johns
Hopkins University. Their home
is only a five-minute walk from
Ru Chih's office.

"That way," Ru Chih told her children, "I can spend extra hours each day with the family and the work I love, instead of in a car, a subway, or a bus!"

Ru Chih is doing research on how a disease called cancer gets started. She is finding out how cells in the body grow old. Understanding how cells are born, how they live, grow old, and die is called molecular biology. Through her research, she will learn more about the way people grow old.

Because she is such a fine scientist and teacher, Dr. Ru Chih Cheo Huang was promoted to the rank of professor. This is the highest position a teacher can hold in a college. Ru Chih is the first woman to be a professor in

the science department at The
Johns Hopkins University.

Ru Chih is very happy with her life as a mother, a wife, and a scientist. Her research is respected by scientists all over the world.

Sometimes students come to Ru Chih for advice about their careers. She tells them what she learned when she was a little girl.

"Don't wait for someone else to tell you that you can succeed. Believe in yourself. And *make your own plans.*

"Always keep a clear path open to your goal. In walking along that path," says Dr. Ru Chih Cheo Huang, "you will find that life can be a joyful journey."